THE XINGYI
BOXING MANUAL

THE XINGYI
BOXING MANUAL

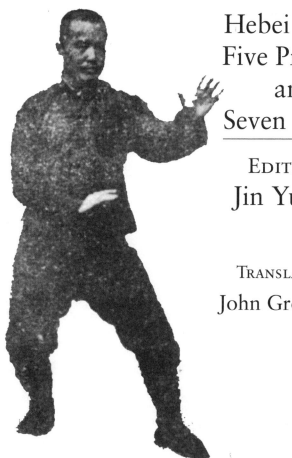

Hebei Style's
Five Principles
and
Seven Words

EDITED BY
Jin Yunting

TRANSLATED BY
John Groschwitz

BLUE SNAKE BOOKS
BERKELEY, CALIFORNIA

Published by Blue Snake Books

Blue Snake Books' publications are distributed by
North Atlantic Books
P.O. Box 12327
Berkeley, California 94712

Cover and text design by Susan Quasha
Printed in the United States of America

The Xingyi Boxing Manual is sponsored by the Society for the Study of Native Arts and Sciences, a nonprofit educational corporation whose goals are to develop an educational and cross-cultural perspective linking various scientific, social, and artistic fields; to nurture a holistic view of arts, sciences, humanities, and healing; and to publish and distribute literature on the relationship of mind, body, and nature.

North Atlantic Books' publications are available through most bookstores. For further information, visit our websites at www.northatlanticbooks.com and www.bluesnakebooks.com or call 800-733-3000.

PLEASE NOTE: The creators and publishers of this book disclaim any liabilities for loss in connection with following any of the practices, exercises, and advice contained herein. To reduce the chance of injury or any other harm, the reader should consult a professional before undertaking this or any other martial arts, movement, meditative arts, health, or exercise program. The instructions and advice printed in this book are not in any way intended as a substitute for medical, mental, or emotional counseling with a licensed physician or healthcare provider.

Library of Congress Cataloging-in-Publication Data

Xing yi quan pu wu gang qi yan lun. English.
  The xingyi boxing manual : Hebei style's five principles and seven words / Edited by Jin Yunting ; translated by John Groschwitz.
    p. cm.
Includes bibliographical references.
  ISBN 1-55643-473-1
  1. Hand to hand fighting, Oriental. 2. Martial arts—China. I. Jin, Yunting. II. Title.
  GV1112 .X5613 2003
  796.8—dc22

2003022057

2 3 4 5 6 7 VERSA 14 13 12 11

To Naoko,
for pushing me in the right direction.

Acknowledgments

The publication of this translation would not have been possible without the help and guidance of many people. Thanks go first to my teachers, for their willingness to share their arts. Annie Chang of U.C. Berkeley's Center for Chinese Studies Library has provided help with translation of difficult passages, and Wu Yifeng, Guo Kaichun, and the rest of the staff have provided abundant research help. Conversations with Master Liang Kequan of Beijing during 2000 yielded a great deal of background information that has influenced my approach to this material; for his insight and instruction I am deeply grateful.

I am indebted to Dan Miller, who graciously granted permission to reprint the photos on the cover and pages 56, 61, and 62. I am grateful to Kathy Glass, who carefully and quickly edited the final draft; and special thanks go to Jess O'Brien at North Atlantic Books, who has managed the project with incredible patience and seen it through to completion.

Contents

CALLIGRAPHY FROM THE ORIGINAL EDITION. IT READS (R TO L):
Mid-autumn, guihai year [1923],
"Skill approaching the Dao*"*
Sheng Shengyi of Wujin

CALLIGRAPHY FROM THE ORIGINAL EDITION. IT READS (R TO L):
[To] the great athlete Yunting
"The path to health"
Sheng Shengyi

PHOTO FROM THE ORIGINAL EDITION. UPPER CAPTION:
Photo of Jin Yunting at age forty-three

LOWER CAPTION:
Calligraphy by Jin Bianshi of Jiading
The fifth month, guihai year [1923]

無事之家不知其福也
事至始知無事之福矣
無病之身不知其樂也
病生始知無病之樂矣

CALLIGRAPHY FROM THE ORIGINAL EDITION BY JIN YUNTING. IT READS:
The person without troubles does not recognize their prosperity;
When trouble arrives, then one begins to know the prosperity
of being worry-free.
The body without sickness does not recognize its happiness;
When sickness arises, then one begins to know the happiness of
being healthy.

THE XINGYI
BOXING MANUAL

Translator's Preface

THIS TRANSLATION is the result of a fortuitous accident. While combing through piles of martial arts books and manuals in search of other material, I unexpectedly stumbled upon this unique book by Jin Yunting and knew immediately that it must be rendered into English. Originally published in 1931, this slim volume combines the basic "songs" of Xingyi's postures, the images and concepts associated with each element, and the guidelines for practice contained in the "seven words," along with images of Jin himself in each posture. Coming directly from an eighth-generation practitioner of a famous lineage, it represents an important link to classical boxing and is a unique record of Xingyi boxing at the beginning of the Republican era. As the senior student of Shang Yunxiang and, as he states in his preface, also a student of Sun Lutang, Jin Yunting was in a unique position. He was able to draw not only on his own experience with these two great teachers, but also on insight gained from their studies with Guo Yunshen and Li Cunyi, both renowned for their Xingyi skills. This work, then, is certainly a distillation of the knowledge and experience of many of the major figures in the history of Xingyi boxing and, as such, deserves study and contemplation.

The first part of the present book is comprised of the original material by Jin Yunting and, except for the reordering of some calligraphic plates, appears in the same sequence as when first published. Following this I have added a partial lineage chart, graphically representing Jin Yunting's lineage, as well as biographies for those wishing to have more background on these figures. Some portions of this translation are similar to translations found elsewhere; however, I have tried to elucidate certain passages that were heretofore ambiguous or confusing, and have endeavored to translate the entire text with an eye toward readability and clarity.

When needed, notes are provided to clarify a specific point, though I have sought to keep these to a minimum. The Chinese terms *Xingyi* and *Xinyi*, instead of Form-Intention and Mind-Intention, are in common usage among most practitioners and have thus been retained throughout the text. Certain other terms, mostly related to Chinese medicine, have also been left in the original for clarity's sake, with accompanying references. All terms in the book are romanized according to the *pinyin* system, and all Chinese names are written according to the Chinese system, i.e., last name first, with characters for the names of Xingyi practitioners following their first occurrence in the text.

The material in this book represents the essential aspects of Xingyi practice as developed and refined over generations and, while not a substitute for a good teacher, it is an essential adjunct to any serious study of this art. As Cui Heqing states in his foreword: "When drinking water, one must ponder its source." We should consider what is contained in these few pages and attempt to understand and analyze its meaning. The more clearly we can understand the classic texts, comparing their alternate versions and styles, the more easily we will be able to seek the subtleties of this profound art. It is my hope that this translation allows the true intent of *The Xingyi Boxing Manual* to be readily understood by the general Xingyi practitioner, and that it furthers understanding of this art's martial and healing aspects. I have done my utmost to translate these passages faithfully, clearly, and according to their original meaning. Any mistakes contained herein are entirely my own, and I welcome any comments or corrections.

John Groschwitz
Berkeley, April 2003

Foreword by Qian Yantang

IN THE PAST, my father was a government official in the capital county. Now, it's known that northerners possess a very stubborn temperament, especially martial artists. When I was young I followed him to his post, and in my spare time, apart from hard studies, I enjoyed martial skill. Springy legs, Shaolin, spear, lance, sword, and halberd—there was nothing I was not adept at. Later I met Guo Yunshen of Shen County, Hebei Province, who said to me, "Rather than exert yourself with these lesser arts, why don't you devote your strength to a true teaching?" I then invited him to our residence with all the gifts appropriate for a teacher so that I might seek stillness in movement and achieve a superior level of fighting skill. After more than ten years of study, I suddenly realized that I had developed considerable *qi* and had received a considerable gift, and that his words were truly not empty. Now, though I have already passed middle age, my spirit is exceptional, and I feel contented. After returning south to live in Shanghai, I unexpectedly encountered Jin Yunting of Wuqiao, with whom I discussed this boxing art. I discovered that he was of the same lineage as myself, and after thoroughly questioning his origins, found that he was the prominent student of Shang Yunxiang of Leling County, Shandong Province. He is currently a guest of Sheng Zecheng of Wujin, who nearly a year ago invited him to teach at his residence, where the number of those who come to study and benefit from this art has increased daily. Now, Yunting has illuminated the various postures of Xingyi using photo-reproduction and amended basic explanations so that later practitioners may all receive the true teachings of this style, and all people may benefit and lengthen their life. As this book nears completion, I recount its origins with these simple words.

Autumn's Eve, *guihai* year [1923]
Qian Yantang [錢硯堂] of Hang County

Foreword by Sheng Jun

A SIDE FROM the cultivation of virtue and the cultivation of wisdom, I also value the cultivation of the body. There are many paths to cultivation of the body, but if you are seeking one that is simple and suitable for all ages, there is none like Xingyi boxing, because this art specifically takes *qi* cultivation as its foundation. Splitting, Smashing, Drilling, Pounding, and Crossing correspond to metal, wood, water, fire, and earth and divide externally into the five postures. Internally they fill the five organs and are the natural, profound way to health. Now Jin Yunting of Wuqiao is using these illustrations to demonstrate clearly, at great advantage to later generations, how easy it is! I began studying this art with Mr. Jin Yunting during the winter of the *xinyou* year [1921], and in less than twenty months I already feel that my body is strong and healthy through its [Xingyi's] exceptional protective benefits. I greatly look forward to the publishing and wide dissemination of this book, and cannot control my fervent wishes that numerous future students may research this physical cultivation and enter onto this right path.

Written the fifth month, *guihai* year [1923]
Sheng Jun [盛 鈞], Style-name Weichen [蔚 岑], of Wu County
Sixty-three years of age

Foreword by Zheng Guangzhao

AFTER THE REFORMS of the *xinhai* year [the 1911 revolution], I moved to Shanghai to teach at the residence of Guardian[1] Sheng. There I met Mr. Jin Yunting of Wuqiao, who told me he had come from the north and was skilled in martial arts. I had no experience with this art, and my nature was not one to be drawn to these things, so I dismissed this and put it behind me. Now Mr. Wu Dicheng, pen-named Zhiting, and Mr. Lü Zibin both had stiff weak bodies, but after studying for just more than one year, they felt that their body and *qi* were both truly changed. Because Dicheng and the others all realized Xingyi's efficacious nature, they recommended it to Mr. Cui Heqing. When his chronic asthma and exhausted body began to heal, he hastened his efforts and, in less than a year, all of his maladies had disappeared.

I found this quite remarkable and said to our teacher that he was not only good at fighting arts, but also skilled in healing arts. In answer, our teacher lectured us, saying: "All of the martial arts in the world originated with Damo. Yue Wumu[2] of the Song Dynasty looked back to and combined the essence of the two classics written by Damo—the *Muscle-Tendon Changing Classic* and the *Marrow-Washing Classic*—to create Xingyi boxing. No matter whether you look at it straightforward or roundabout, complicated or confused, it all comes down to using the intention to create form, and using form to create *qi*. This is the essence of what I have learned.

"When I was young I engaged in business, and my body became weak and I had many illnesses. I was told that if I could obtain the teachings of Xingyi boxing, I could eradicate this weakness and illness, so I began searching for a teacher. Now, while those who are skilled in Shaolin or Wudang arts are numerous, very few are skilled at Xingyi. Those who do know, if they are not arrogant, are tight-lipped, so I traveled around and around until I finally reached the two masters, Shang Yunxiang of Leling County and Sun Lutang of Wanping County, under whose guidance I traveled for more than ten years. I was able to glimpse their art, and although my own art is still not refined, my body is now without maladies.

"I tell people that what I say to them is not deception. In fact, there is nothing outside the cultivation of *qi*. If you can nurture *qi*, your mind will be calm, you will be what people call 'a gentleman of heavenly calm and composure,' and your body will have no place for sickness. You say that I am skilled in the healing arts, but I dare not claim so."

I say that this is just my teacher's modesty and that, in fact, his words are a true understanding of the *Dao*, for though I have been associated with him for only several months, I feel that I am flourishing in my everyday life. Now our teacher has followed the requests of his compatriots to publish this volume. I present what I have heard and seen, briefly recounting it here as an addendum to the forewords of these other gentlemen. As for the illustrations and discussions, we have our teacher's original text, so I won't reiterate those here.

Eighth month, *guihai* year [1923]
Zheng Guangzhao [鄭光照], Style-name Yicang [逸蒼], of Wujin
Penned at the Yuzhai Study, Shanghai
Sixty-three years of age

Foreword by Sheng Yulin

XINGYI BOXING is also called *Wuxing*[3] boxing and follows the principles of metal, wood, water, fire, and earth; heart, liver, spleen, lungs, kidney, yin and yang; and movement and stillness. Not only is it an exceptional fighting art, but it also strengthens tendons and bones and enlivens the blood and vessels. Formerly I was plump and my movements hindered. Mr. Jin has trained me for two winters and summers without cease, and I now feel that my spirit is lively and my gait light and easy, proving that this boxing art has endless advantage for people in terms of physical cultivation. It should be regarded by all people as a great treasure. I submit these few words of record as accompaniment to the text.

Sheng Yulin [盛玉麐] of Wujin

Foreword by Cui Heqing

XINGYI BOXING is truly the essential art of physical cultivation. Practice requires perseverance, but if one practices daily without cease, power will fill the body and the results will exceed expectations. Before, I suffered from damp phlegm and shortness of breath which medicine could not help. Many of my comrades recommended this art to me, and I took to the learning of Mr. Yunting, a man of sincere heart. After only one year, my body is now light and healthy, my vision and appetite superb. When drinking water one should ponder its source. Truly this has been a gift from my teacher, so I write these few lines in appreciation of his superior conduct, and as a record, so that it will not be forgotten.

**Written by Cui Heqing [崔鶴卿] of Wuqing, near the Capital
Fifty-seven years of age**

Foreword by Wu Shulan

M Y BODY is thin but my spirit is fierce. In the winter of the *renzi* year [1912], I traveled north and suddenly developed a pulmonary hemorrhage. By the time this sickness healed, it had greatly injured my *yuan qi*.[4] With physical exertion I was winded, and medicine had no effect. This went on for several years, and although I was not old, I was already exhausted. This was very distressing.

Mr. Jin Yunting was a friend of mine from the same hometown, skilled in the art of Xingyi. In the seventh month of the *jiwei* year [1919], he came to Shanghai and expounded to me the mysteries of this art, which takes the creation of freely downward-flowing *qi* as its main principle. After filling fully *Dantian*, one can supplement deficiencies of both pre- and post-heaven *qi*. If one studies this art, then one can receive the most benefits. Mr. Jin expounded most highly and I suddenly saw the light. Following, I met with Mr. Wu Dicheng and Mr. Lü Zibin and, in the ninth month of that year, I began studying.

Mr. Jin was skilled in giving systematic explanation and always taught without reserve. I trained continuously without cease, several times a day, and in less than five years, my old illness had been eradicated. Now I am fifty-two, and my body is more healthy than before. My steps are as lively as those of a forty-year-old. As for Misters Wu and Lü, their health was originally better than mine and now is even stronger. With deep feeling I recount this and, with these few words, record it so that it will not be forgotten.

> The fifth month, *guihai* year [1923]
> Wu Shulan [吳樹蘭], Pen-name Zhiting [芷庭], of Nangong, Hebei

Foreword by Wu Dicheng

XINGYI BOXING originated with Damo, passed to Yue Wumu of the Song Dynasty, and during the great Ming period experienced continuous transmission, with branches spreading in abundance throughout the north. Even I had heard of it. Jin Yunting of Wuqiao is skilled in this art. In the autumn of the *jiwei* year [1919] he came to Shanghai, and once we met we became inseparable good friends. He then set forth his intention to make the dispelling of sickness and extension of life his goal. I myself had many sicknesses and therefore began studying. After only five winters and summers without cease I felt that, compared to before, my spirit and strength were like those of a completely different person. I then began to believe that Mr. Jin's words were not just exaggeration.

Subsequently I heard that he had a school-brother who gave him the transmissions of their [martial-art] school, which had not yet been made public. I read this, which was on the whole concerned with cultivation of the body, the nurturing of *qi*, and how—if one is able to develop *qi*—the spirit will naturally become complete. I realized that this document is perfect for those who have interest but no way to proceed. Although its meaning is profound, the words are very clear; this art is suitable for young and old alike and helps one to attain benevolence and long life. I encouraged him [Jin Yunting] to publish this book for the benefit of others, and he agreed wholeheartedly. I have respectfully added this colophon of a few words to record something worthy of admiration.

The fifth month, *guihai* year [1923]
Written by Wu Dicheng [吳 砥 成] of Wu County, Jiangsu

Foreword by Lü Zibin

JIN YUNTING is originally from Wuqiao, Hebei Province. As a young man, he studied under the famous teacher Shang Yunxiang and achieved great understanding after more than twenty years of researching Xingyi boxing. This art is divided into five fists: Splitting, which corresponds to metal; Smashing, which corresponds to wood; Drilling, which corresponds to water; Pounding, which corresponds to fire; and Crossing, which corresponds to earth. Its main aim is to nurture *qi* and develop the body, and is unconnected with fighting. It is said that the form circulates the intention; therefore it is called Xingyi. In the autumn of the *jiwei* year [1919], Fourth Master Zecheng began promoting physical education and invited Mr. Jin to Shanghai to teach his comrades. Mr. Jin was not vexed by repeated instruction and, in fact, was as comforting and friendly as a spring wind. I was formerly of weak constitution and always taking medicine, but after engaging in this practice for only a year, it was as if my sicknesses had disappeared. I now benefit from continued good health and deeply believe that the ancient worthies do not deceive us. I discussed with my teacher the possibility of reprinting this boxing treatise for compatriot fellows, and so that this national treasure of physical cultivation can be esteemed by people in the West. I now relate these origins as this printing nears completion.

The fifth month, *guihai* year [1923]
Lü Zibin [呂子彬], Pen-name Wenwei [文蔚], of Ba County,
near the Capital

Foreword by Jin Yunting

MENGZI SAID: "Control your will and do not scatter your *qi*,"[5] because the mind and the *qi* show your inner state. The mind is the commander of the *qi*. The *qi* is the army of the mind. If I am a commander without troops, then when it comes time for battle, who would employ me? No matter what we attempt to do, even when the mind is set, if the *qi* is insufficient, then it must be that matters cannot succeed. Therefore, Mengzi also said: "I'm good at developing my vast *qi*."[6]

As a youth, my constitution was weak, I was often sick, and could not endure physical labor. Some people enjoined me to use Xingyi boxing—which has the main aim of nurturing *qi*—as a restorative method, for if the *qi* is sufficient, the body is healthy and sickness will depart. Accordingly I sought those skilled in this art and found Master Shang Yunxiang of Leling, and Master Sun Lutang of Wanping, under whose guidance I traveled for more than ten years. Not only was my sickness healed, but my constitution became very strong through the exceptional protective benefits of this art.

Xingyi boxing originated with the founding master Damo, and from He'nan came to Beijing. It is simple and uncomplicated, refined and not crude, easily understood, strenuous but not harmful. If practiced daily according to the proper theories, it will quickly cause tight sinews to stretch, the slack to draw in, the separated to unite, and the soft to become firm, and it will enliven the blood and vessels and strengthen the spirit. Needless to say, it may be practiced by both young and old without difficulty. During the autumn of the *jiwei* year [1919], Fourth Master Sheng Zecheng invited me to Shanghai. Those comrades who undertook to research this health-building and nourishing art did not abandon it, gathering together morning and night, and they enjoined me to pass on this method as sustenance for those to come. To avoid seeming ignorant, I attach these few sentences simply to associate myself with men of true skill.

Written by Jin Yunting [靳雲亭], Pen-name Zhenqi [振起], of Wuqiao

THE FIVE PRINCIPLES

Preparatory Posture

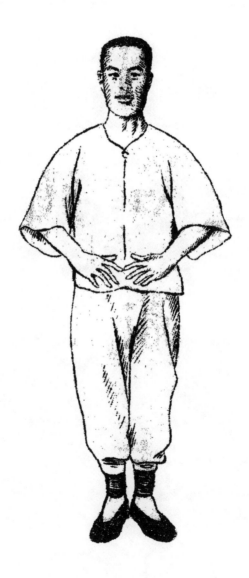

Calm the body and sink the qi
Inhale and open the chest
The intention does not wander
With sincerity of heart, maintain the center

束 身 下 氣
吸 氣 開 胸
意 勿 外 馳
誠 心 守 中

Beneficial in nourishing vast *qi*
Continually intone the Wisdom Sutra[7]
Above, middle, and below the *qi* settles
The body, hands, and feet are aligned and true

善 養 浩 然 氣
多 誦 般 若 經
上 中 下 總 氣 把 定
身 手 足 規 矩 繩 墨

Pi Quan—Splitting Fist

The first is called splitting
Its form is like an axe
It corresponds to the metal element
Of the *zang* organs, it nourishes the lungs

第一日劈
其形似斧
五行屬金
五臟養肺

In use, the fist must drill close
In application, each posture must have *qi*
Do not bend forward or lean back
Do not tilt to the left or slant to the right

用拳要攢緊用把把有氣
不前俯後仰不左斜右歪

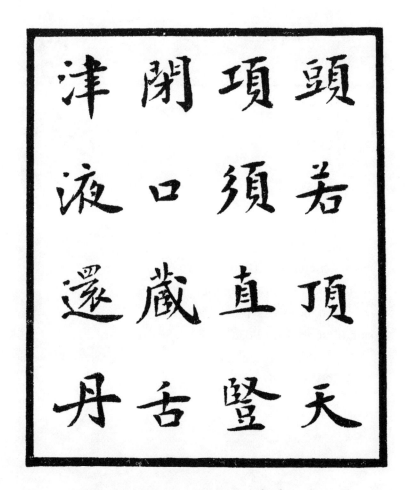

The head seems to press to the heavens
The nape of the neck must be straight and erect
Close the mouth and hide the tongue
So the *jin* and *ye*[8] can return to *Dantian*

Discussion on the Rising and Falling of Splitting Fist
劈拳起落論

The two hands issue from the mouth,
drilling up and out at the level of the brow,
the back fist following closely.
The arms embrace the ribs at the level of the heart,
the *qi* follows the body's movements and sinks to *Dantian*,
as the two hands fall together and the back foot follows.
The fingers are spread, and the tiger's mouth round,
the front arm is at the height of the heart,
the back hand is hidden beneath the ribs.
The tips of the hand, foot, and nose are all in a line,
the small finger is turned up at the level of the brow.
The striking method of Splitting Fist is to drill up,
as the feet and hands fall, the tip of the tongue pushes up,
step forward to change postures and the *yin* hand drops.

兩拳以抱口中去 ＼ 拳前上攢如眉齊
後拳隨跟緊相連 ＼ 兩手抱脇如心齊
氣隨身法落丹田 ＼ 兩手齊落後脚隨
四指分開虎口元 ＼ 前手高秪與心齊
後手只在脇下藏 ＼ 手足鼻尖三對尖
小指翻上如眉齊 ＼ 劈拳打法向上攢
脚手齊落舌尖頂 ＼ 進步換式陰掌落

Beng Quan—Smashing Fist

The second is called smashing
Its form is like an arrow
It corresponds to the wood element
Of the *zang* organs, it calms the liver

第二曰崩
其形似箭
五行屬木
五臟舒肝

The front foot should not hook in and must not turn out
The back foot seems straight, but is not straight;
seems turned out, but is not turned out

前足不宜裡扣不可外橫
後足似順非順似橫不橫

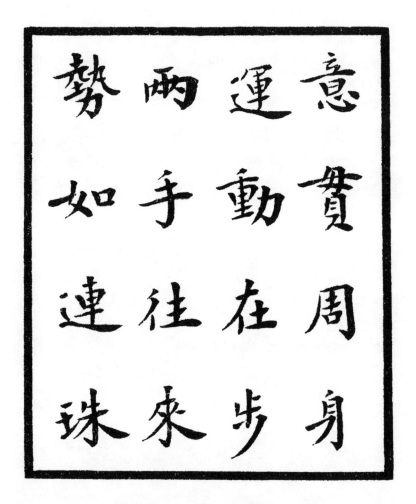

The intention fills the entire body
Movement comes from the feet
The two hands come and go
The postures like a string of pearls

Discussion on the Rising and Falling of Smashing Fist

崩拳起落論

In the Smashing Fist posture, the three tips align,
the tiger's eye[9] faces up, at the level of the heart.
The back *yang* hand is hidden beneath the ribs.
The front foot must be straight; the back foot
turned.
The back foot must be stable, making a V-shape.[10]
When Smashing Fist turns, reach the height of the
brow,
the body stands straight and true as the foot is lifted,
the foot is raised, then strikes out horizontally below the
knee,
the foot and hand fall together into scissor legs,[11]
the front foot turned, the back foot straight.
The striking method of Smashing Fist is to push the
tongue-tip up,
rub and extend above the elbow of the front hand,
advance and issue, first striking the ribs,
the back foot following closely.

崩拳出式三尖對 \ 虎眼朝上如心齊
後手陽拳脇下藏 \ 前脚要順後脚丁
後脚穩要人字形 \ 崩拳翻身望眉齊
身站正直脚提起 \ 脚起膝下横脚跐
脚手齊落剪子步 \ 前脚要横後脚順
崩拳打法舌尖頂 \ 前手攞肘望上托
進步出拳先打脇 \ 後脚是連緊隨跟

Zuan Quan—Drilling Fist

The third is called drilling
Its form is like lightning
It corresponds to the water element
Of the *zang* organs, it supplements the kidneys

第 三 曰 攢
其 形 似 閃
五 行 屬 水
五 臟 補 腎

The two legs and two arms seem straight but are not
    straight;
seem bent, but are not bent
There is *yin* and there is *yang*, but the central *qi* is stable

兩 股 兩 肱 似 直 非 直 似 曲 非 曲
有 陰 有 陽 中 氣 穩 也

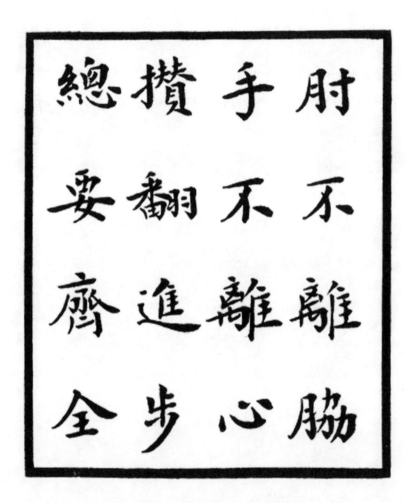

The elbows do not leave the ribs
The hands do not leave the heart
Drill, overturn, and advance
Always uniting the whole

Discussion on the Rising and Falling of Drilling Fist
攢拳起落論

The front *yin* hand hooks downward,
the rear *yang* hand drills upward.
When issuing, drill high at the level of the brow.
The two elbows hug the heart as the back foot rises,
the eyes watch the front hand as the four extremities stop.
When Drilling Fist changes postures, the body moves,
the front foot steps first, the back foot follows,
the back *yin* palm is hidden beneath the elbow;
when setting the foot down, the three points must always align.
The front *yang* hand strikes the tip of the nose,
the little finger turns up, the elbow guards the heart.
The advancing step of Drilling Fist also strikes the tip of the nose,
the front palm hooks with the wrist and crosses downward;
advance as the palms turn, and the striking fist extends.

前手陰掌向下扣 \ 後手陽拳望上攢
出拳高攢如眉齊 \ 兩肘抱心後腳起
眼看前手四稍停 \ 攢拳換式身法動
前腳先步後腳隨 \ 後手陰掌肘下藏
落步總要三尖對 \ 前手陽拳打鼻尖
小指翻上肘護心 \ 攢拳進步打鼻尖
前掌扣腕望下橫 \ 進步掌翻打虎托

Pao Quan—Pounding Fist

The fourth is called pounding
Its form is like a cannon
It corresponds to the fire element
Of the *zang* organs, it nourishes the heart

第四曰炮

其形似炮

五行屬火

五臟養心

If hard then empty and insubstantial; if soft then heavy
    and solid
Heavy and solid like a mountain, the *qi* penetrates the
    flesh

剛則虛浮柔則沈實

沈重如山氣透膚理

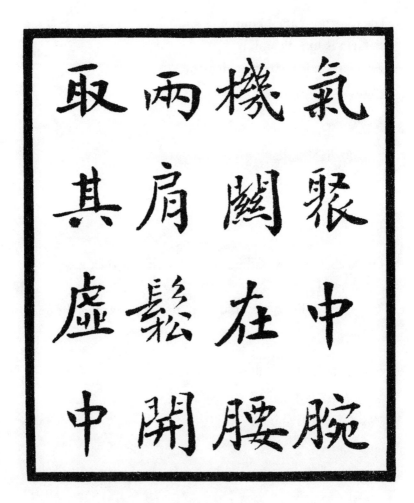

The *qi* gathers as the wrists take the center
The mechanism is in the waist
The two shoulders relax and open
To seek its hollowness

Discussion on the Rising and Falling of Pounding Fist
炮拳起落論

The two elbows gather closely as the foot lifts up,
the two hands move together like a *yang* fist,
the front hand moves transversely, the back hand straight,
the two fists gather at the level of the navel,
the *qi* follows the body's movements and enters *Dantian*.
When the feet and hands fall together, the three tips align.
The fist strikes at the height of the heart,
the tiger's eye of the front hand presses up,
the back fist drills up at the height of the brow,
the tiger's eye faces down and the elbow sinks.
The striking method of Pounding Fist is to lift the foot;
as the foot sets down, the front fist drills up.
The hands and feet fall together in a crossing step,[12]
the back foot following closely.

両肘緊抱脚提起 ＼ 兩拳一緊要陽拳
前手要橫後手丁 ＼ 兩拳高衹肚臍抱
氣就身法入丹田 ＼ 脚手齊落三尖對
拳打高衹與心齊 ＼ 前手虎眼朝上頂
後拳上攢眉上齊 ＼ 虎眼朝下肘下垂
炮拳打法脚提起 ＼ 落步前拳望上攢
拳脚齊落十字步 ＼ 後脚是連緊隨橫

Heng Quan—Crossing Fist

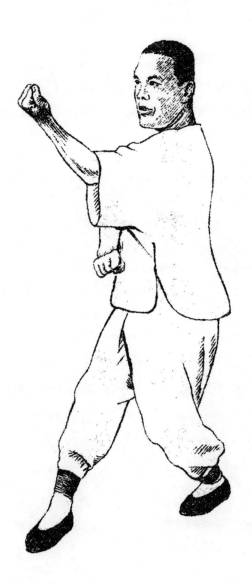

The fifth is called crossing
Its form is like a spring
It corresponds to the earth element
Of the *zang* organs, it nourishes the spleen

第五曰橫

其形似彈

五行屬土

五臟養脾

Twist the body with the footwork; the shape is like
    twisted yarn
The inside opening and the outside closing is called
    closing the chest

扭身要步形同擰繩

內開外合是謂扣胸

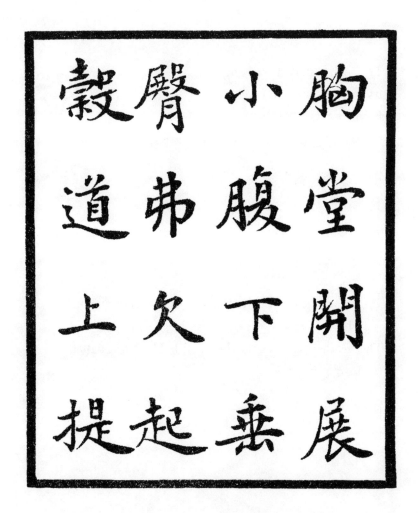

The chest cavity expands
The abdomen sinks
The buttocks do not rise up
And the anus is lifted

Discussion on the Rising and Falling of Crossing Fist
橫拳起落論

The front hand is *yang*, the back hand is *yin*,
the back hand is hidden beneath the elbow.
In changing postures and issuing, the foot rises up,
the body method is to stand unified so the *qi* can circulate,
the tongue-tip curls up and the *qi* issues forth.
Crossing Fist changes postures with scissor legs,[13]
angle the body with the step, then the foot and hands fall,
the rear hand turns to *yang* and pulls out.
When setting the foot down, the *yang* hand and three tips align,
the tip of the nose and tip of the foot follow closely.
The striking method of Crossing Fist makes the back fist *yin*,
the front is *yang*, and its elbow protects the heart.
Draw the bow to the left and right, pulling to the outside;
when the feet and hands fall together, the tongue-tip curls.

前手陽拳後手陰 ＼ 後手只在肘下藏
換式出手脚提起 ＼ 身法一站氣能通
舌尖上攢氣外發 ＼ 橫拳換式剪子股
斜身要步脚手落 ＼ 後手翻陽望外撥
落步陽拳三尖對 ＼ 鼻尖脚尖緊相連
橫拳打法後拳陰 ＼ 前手陽拳肘護心
左右開弓望外撥 ＼ 脚手齊落舌尖捲

THE SEVEN WORDS

The Seven Words and Twenty-One Methods of Xingyi Boxing

形意拳七字二十一法

Ding—Pressing

The three pressings:

The head presses upward.

The tongue presses against the palate.

The hands press outward.

To clearly understand the three pressings brings power.

三頂者

頭望上頂

舌尖頂上嗓

手掌望外頂

明了三頂多一力

Kou—Hooking

The three hookings:

The edges of the shoulders must hook.

The backs of the palms must hook.

The soles of the feet must hook downward.

To clearly understand the three hooks brings refinement.

三扣者

膀尖要扣

手背要扣

脚面要望下扣

明了三扣多一精

Yuan—Rounding

The three roundings:
The spine must round.
The chest must round.
The tiger's mouth must round.
To clearly understand the three rounds brings subtlety.

三元者
脊背要元
胸脯要元
虎口要元
明了三元多一妙

Bao—Holding

The three holdings:
Dantian must hold *qi* as the root.
The mind must hold the body as its focus.
The arms must hold the integration of the four limbs.
To clearly understand the three holdings brings
movement.

三抱
丹田要抱氣為根
心中要抱身為主
胳膊要抱四稍停
明了三抱多一行

Chui—Falling

The three fallings:

The *qi* falls to *Dantian* for the body to be the principle.

The edges of the shoulders fall so the intention is pure.

The elbows fall for the shoulders to be the root.

To clearly understand the three fallings brings cleverness.

三垂

氣垂丹田身為主

膀尖下垂意為真

肘尖下垂肩為根

明了三垂多一靈

Yue—Arcing

The three arcings:

The arms must arc like a bow.

The wrists must arc pressing outward.

The legs must curve in a connected arc.

To clearly understand the three arcings brings power.

三月芽者

胳膊似弓要月芽

手腕外頂要月芽

腿月曲連灣要月芽

明了三月多一力

Ting—Integrating
The three integrations:
The neck must be integrated in a vertical direction.
The body's movement must be integrated to differentiate
    the four directions.
The legs and knees must be integrated below like the
    roots of a tree.
To clearly understand the three integrations brings ability.

停

三停

脖梗要停有豎相

身法要停分四面

腿膝下停如樹根

明了三停多一法

Though the seven body methods are divided three by
seven, the twenty-one methods are all one method.

總身七法又分三七,二十一法是一法也

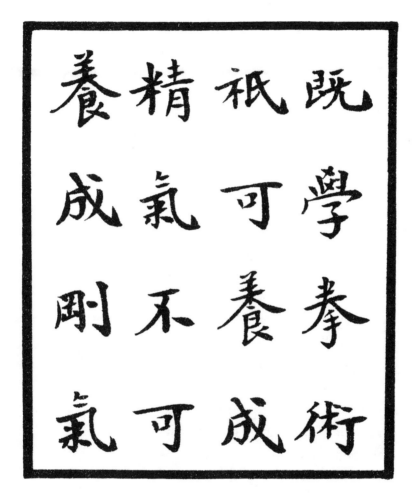

CALLIGRAPHY FROM THE ORIGINAL EDITION BY JIN YUNTING.
IT READS:
When studying boxing, one must only develop essential qi;
One must not develop hard qi.

The Essential Points of Xingyi Boxing's Six Harmonies and the Extremities
形意拳六合百體要領

The mind harmonizes with the intention;
the intention harmonizes with the *qi*;
the *qi* harmonizes with the power;
these are the three internal harmonies.
The hands harmonize with the feet;
the elbows harmonize with the knees;
the shoulders harmonize with the hips;
these are the three external harmonies.
These together are called the six harmonies.
The left hand harmonizes with the right foot;
the left elbow harmonizes with the right knee;
the left shoulder harmonizes with the right hip,
and conversely so on the right side.
The head harmonizes with the hands;
the hands harmonize with the body;
the body harmonizes with the footwork.
Are these not also external harmonies?
The mind harmonizes with the eyes;
the liver harmonizes with the tendons;
the spleen harmonizes with the muscles;
the lungs harmonize with the body;
the kidneys harmonize with the bones;
Are these not also internal harmonies?

Are there then truly only six harmonies? Actually, these
only describe the constituent parts. In the end, if one
moves, then there are none that do not move; if one
harmonizes, then there are none that do not harmonize.
The five elements and the head, torso, and four limbs can
be known from this.

心與意合 ＼ 意與氣合 ＼ 氣與力合 ＼ 内三合也

手與足合 ＼ 肘與膝合 ＼ 肩與胯合 ＼ 外三合也

此謂六合

左手與右足相合 ＼ 左肘與右膝相合 ＼ 左肩與右胯相合

右之與左亦然

以及頭與手合 ＼ 手與身合 ＼ 身與步合 ＼ 孰非外合

心與眼合 ＼ 肝與筋合 ＼ 脾與肉合 ＼ 肺與身合

腎與骨合 ＼ 孰非内合

豈但六合而已哉

然此特分而言之也 ＼ 總之一動而無不動一合而無不合

五行百骸悉在其中矣

Afterword by Sheng Linhuai

I HAVE HAD A SIMPLE INTEREST IN XINGYI, but until now I have never pursued it. Fourth nephew Zecheng sought Yunting's art and brought him to Shanghai. In only a few months, followers thronged his doors, and fourth nephew was elated. Now all comrades and gentlemen throughout the world may benefit from these pictures and descriptions. In appreciation of Instructor Yunting's guidance, I attach this colophon.

Autumn, *guihai* year [1923]
Sheng Linhuai [盛 麟 懷] of Wujin

LINEAGE BIOGRAPHIES

Jin Yunting's Xingyi Lineage

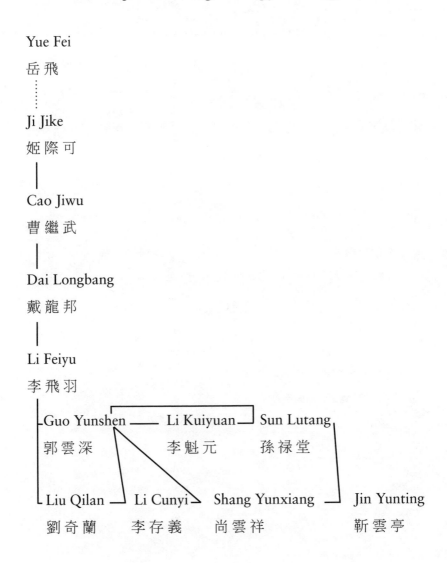

Note on the Biographies

THE BIOGRAPHIES on the following pages are translated from the *Encyclopedia of Chinese Martial Arts*, published in 1998. Included here are all the main figures in Jin Yunting's Xingyi lineage beginning with the purported originator Yue Fei, with the exceptions of Li Kuiyuan and Jin himself, for whom no entries existed. These biographies are presented "as is," with all quotations and parenthetical notes following the original format. Obvious errata have been left unaltered, but footnoted where possible. Though ostensibly designed to serve as authoritative biographies, the *Encyclopedia* lists no sources for the facts and quotations therein, and no methodology for the collection of data. For now, readers should seek to compare these with the various other existing biographies, until more energy can be devoted to compiling thoroughly researched histories of these figures.

Translator

Biography of Yue Fei 岳飛
(1103–1142)

F AMOUS SONG DYNASTY anti-Jin general and people's hero. Pen-
named Pengju [鵬 舉]. Originally from Tangyin in Xiangzhou
(present-day Tangyin County, He'nan Province). His family was
extremely poor, and as a youth he worked with his father doing farm
work by day and then studying by night, not sleeping until the late
hours. He was fond of reading *Master Zuo's Spring and Autumn
Annals* and admired Sun Wu's *Art of War*.

Even as a young man Yue Fei was full of integrity and possessed
a heart blooming with "the promise of loyalty and righteousness to
country." Under the military leader Zhou Tong and famous spearman
Chen Guang, he studied and attained the essentials of martial arts
and deployment of troops. When not yet an adult, Yue could already
draw a 300-*jin*[14] bow and eight-*dan*[15] crossbow, and was skilled in
the arts of archery and spear. He could shoot left- and right-handed;
his martial skills exceeded all others; and he was "without peer in
the county."

At the end of the Northern Song Dynasty, beginning when Yue was
nineteen, he enlisted in the military four times. The first time he was
the "Captain of ten squads" but resigned upon his father's death.
Later, he became a Chariot-Brigade Commander and determinedly
led his troops into enemy territory, where they encountered a large
enemy force and were scattered, forcing him to return home alone.
During a high tide of national defense, he enlisted for the third time.
Due to his skilled organization of remote pacification troops and his
abilities in arms, he received a promotion to Trusted Gentleman.
Later, because he met the enemy on ice and soundly defeated the Jin
army, Yue was promoted to Gentleman Consultant, a lower-ranking
military officer.

At the beginning of the second year of the *jingkang* reign period (1127), under the leadership of Vice-Marshal Zong Ze, Yue was victorious against Jin troops many times. At the battle of Caozhou (northwest of present-day Cao County, Shandong Province) Yue took the lead in attacking the enemy troops, again soundly defeating the Jin army, this time chasing them for many miles in their retreat and cutting down still more of their soldiers. In deploying troops, Yue Fei advocated that "the cleverness of implementation is contained in one's mind," and that, after sizing up the situation and seizing the opportunity to move cleverly, "if the troops are skilled, and the general strong, then you can use one to stop ten." He was praised by Zong Ze, who proclaimed: "You are brave, wise, and talented, and are unsurpassed by even the great generals of old."

In the same year, the Emperors Huizong and Qinzong were kidnapped, and Zhao Gou seized the opportunity to ascend the throne as Gaozong. Gaozong did not heed the opposition of many of his ministers, relying only on the capitulationists, and moved the capital to Yangzhou, later establishing a new capital at Lin'an (present-day Hangzhou, Zhejiang Province.) Yue Fei was by nature honest and straightforward, and wholly devoted to saving the common people. Although his position was low, and his words carried little weight, he still wrote an appeal to the emperor. In several thousand words he strongly requested to retake Bianjing (present-day Kaifeng, He'nan Province) and regain He'nan, and he resolutely opposed the court's retreat to the south. In the end, because of his "inappropriate words beyond the duties of a minor official," Yue was removed from his post. Because of his strong desire to serve his country, he thereupon sought the assistance of the patriot general Zhang Suo, Bandit-Suppression Commissioner of Hebei Province, who appointed Yue a commander in the central army and later promoted him to Commander-General, a mid-level military officer. Yue was stern and careful in governing his army and viewed martial training and the strict pursuit of refinement and skill as the keys to the employment of troops. Because of this, there was not a battle that his "Yue Family troops" did not win. In the midst of one fierce battle, he seized the great Jin banner, personally captured the Jin general Tuobayewu, and stabbed to death the Jin Commander Heifengdawang. During the battle to guard Bianjing, he shot his bow with his left hand while wielding a lance in his right, crisscrossing through the enemy troops, who were thrown into great chaos and soundly defeated. When the Jin army caught wind of him, they would lose their resolve and exclaim in sorrow, "To move a mountain is easy; to move the Yue army is difficult."

Yue personally took part in one hundred and twenty battles, and his fighting skill was awe-inspiring. His grandson Yue He said: "My forefather observed 'three strictnesses' in governing his army. First, he strictly controlled his forces. He valued selectiveness, once using five hundred of his best soldiers to defeat Wu Shu's 50,000-man Jin army. He also was cautious in training, and between battles took every chance to train his troops, wearing heavy armor to scale walls and cross moats just as in actual battle. He was fair in reward and punishment; when his adopted son Yue Yun did not take training seriously and his horse subsequently lost its front shoe, Yue Fei assigned him one hundred lashes as punishment. He created clear command signals that were simple and readily apparent, so that when the signal was issued, his orders were carried out. He observed strict discipline, stating that he would 'freeze to death before breaking into houses (not forcing his troops into people's homes), starve to death before plundering and seizing.' He set himself as the example, never committing even the smallest infraction. He ate and bivouacked together with his soldiers, sharing their same fortunes and misfortunes. When a soldier was injured, he would personally mix medicine for him. If a soldier sacrificed himself, he would provide for his remaining relatives. Rewards were handed out to all, and he did not keep any for himself.

"Secondly, he strictly controlled his household. He considered farming and study his primary concerns. He did not seek to take advantage of others' power and influence, and did not seek personal gain and positions. If his son performed a military feat, he would not petition for reward and would refuse any that was offered. His residence was thrifty and frugal, he wore only simple clothes and seldom ate meat, and he restrained himself, striving for filial piety and adherence to the Dao, never forgetting his mother's training to 'serve the country with true sincerity.'

"Thirdly, he strictly controlled himself. He did not covet wealth nor put aside farming. He was not attached to lust and kept a household without concubines. He did not brag, and he used his land to support the destitute families of deceased soldiers and his poorer relatives."

The Emperor rewarded Yue Fei with military landholdings and would not accept his request to retire, believing that "if scholar-ministers do not love money, and martial-ministers do not pity death, then all is right in the world." He was successively conferred with the titles Military Revenues Commissioner of the Army for Frontier Pacification, Dynasty-Founding Marquis of Wuchang Commandery, Junior Guardian, Defender-in-Chief, and Bandit-Suppression Commissioner of the North and South.

In the ninth year of the *shaoxing* reign period (1139) Gaozong, fearing the Jin, willingly "moved to the left of the river" and with the traitorous minister Qin Kuai strongly advocated for peace negotiations with the Jin. Yue Fei again submitted a petition fiercely opposing this. The next year, the great Jin army led by Wu Shu attacked He'nan. Yue Fei again led his soldiers in counter-attack, greatly defeating the Jin army at the cities of Yan and Yingchang (present-day Xuchang, He'nan Province) and recaptured Zhengzhou and Luoyang. He then led his troops to Zhuxian township, with his vanguard drawing near Bianjing and continuously pounding towards the enemy's center. Hearing of this, the people's militia of the two rivers rose up to join him. At this time, Gaozong and Qin Kuai, with treacherous hearts, bent to the Jin demand that "Yue Fei must die in order to sign a treaty" and, surprisingly, in one day sent twelve golden tablets (imperial edicts) instructing him to retreat.

Yue Fei dejectedly returned to Lin'an, and that night he was stripped of his military powers and given the new title Vice-Commissioner of Military Affairs. Not long after, he was framed for plotting rebellion and imprisoned. Preferring death to capitulation, he stopped eating. In the eleventh year of the *shaoxing* reign period, on the twenty-ninth of the twelfth lunar month (January 27, 1142), on unnecessary and false charges, Yue Fei, his adopted son Yue Yun, and his General-Assistant

Zhang Xuan were executed. As he drew near the execution ground, he wrote on his deposition, "One day heaven will vindicate me! One day heaven will vindicate me!"

Twenty years later, Xiaozong Zhao Shen assumed the throne and, in order to calm the anger of the people, encouraged soldiers to resist the enemy and finally settled Yue Fei's unjust sentence. His body was exhumed with all the according ceremonies and re-buried in Xixialingluan in Hangzhou, with his son Yue Yun at his side. The burial plot was named the "Garden of Essential Loyalty." In the sixth year of the *qiando* reign period (1170) the "Loyal Exemplars Temple" was built in his honor in Ezhou (present-day Wuchang, Hubei Province). In the sixth year of the *chunxi* reign period (1179) Yue was posthumously named Wumu [武穆], and in the fourth year of Ningzong's *jiatai* reign period (1204) he was posthumously granted the title Prince of E [Ezhou, above]. In the first year of Lizong's *baoqing* reign period, Yue's posthumous name was changed to Zhongwu [忠武] and *Prince Yue Zhongwu's Posthumously Collected Writings* was published. His poems and essays were impassioned and filled with the strong feelings of love of country. His representative work, the ode "The Whole River is Red," is a passionate rousing work that shines as bright as the sun and moon.

According to legend, the martial creations by Yue Fei include Yue-style Connected Boxing, *The Xingyi Boxing Manual*, Yue-style Boxing (ten sets), Yue-style Spear, Hooked Spear, Double Sickles, and Double Hammers, among others. Their characteristics are: the postures are short and simple, the stances sink, and the footwork is stable. They move with unexpected crashing and shaking, and use shouts to carry the *qi*. They contain many hand techniques and fewer leg techniques, all without embellishment. The spear arts are sturdy and straightforward, using many straight thrusts to the five directions, as well as slipping thrusts; they do not perform flowery movements in the air, but value fighting and actual use, with strong counter-offensive abilities. One example is the hooked spear, which was specifically designed to fight against the Jin army's "Heavy-Armored Infantry" and "Cane-Head Cavalry."[16, 17]

Biography of Ji Jike 姬際可
(1602–1680)

MARTIAL ARTS PRACTITIONER and founder of Xingyi boxing. Pen-named Longfeng [龍峰], also written Longfeng [龍鳳]. Originally from Puzhou (present-day Yongji County), Hebei Province. According to the preface of Master Li's *Six Harmonies Boxing Manual* (Qing *yongzheng* reign period, 1723–1735), the preface to Wang Zicheng's *Queries on the Boxing Treatise,* and section two of the hand-copied *Ji Family Lineage Manual* (*qianlong* reign period, 1736–1795), Ji Jike was the ninth generation of the Ji family, a family of means, and from an early age he studied literature and martial arts. His skill and bravery were unsurpassed, and he was especially adept in use of the large spear. Like "a flying horse touching the rafters," he was untouchable after raising his spear and was thus called "Heavenly Spear." In order to adapt to the needs of unarmed self-defense, Jike used the theory of his spear skills as the basis of his theory of boxing, and additionally studied the cleverness of animals' fighting.

He obtained the *Six Harmonies Boxing Classic* by Yue Wumu and researched its concepts diligently for ten years. Using the six harmonies as a methodological base, with the five elements and the ten animals as forms, and considering the mind's causation of movement as intention and the intention's ability as boxing skill, Ji created "the six postures of both front and back." These are the concepts of Xinyi Six Harmonies Boxing that: "the mind harmonizes with the intention; the intention harmonizes with the *qi*; the *qi* harmonizes with the force; the hands harmonize with the feet; the elbows harmonize with the knees; the shoulders harmonize with the hips." People called this art "Jike Boxing."

According to legend, after his *qi* was developed, Ji made a visit to the Shaolin Temple at Mt. Song (some say that he resided at Shaolin Temple for ten years, and there he used the techniques of Shaolin's Five Styles of Boxing to create his art), then passed on his art in Luoyang, He'nan Province, and Guichi, Anhui Province. After ten years he returned to his hometown to teach his descendants.

In his later years, Ji defeated roving bandits to the west of his village, killing the bandit leader, and he became known as "Heavenly Spear." He was praised throughout the township, and after his passing, his descendants placed his image in the "Hall of Tribute to Forebears." His disciples are numerous. Wang Yaolong [王耀龍] and Cao Jiwu [曹繼武] are among the most famous.[18]

Biography of Cao Jiwu 曹繼武
(1669–?)

ONE OF THE PRINCIPAL TRANSMITTERS of Xingyi boxing. Also called Riwei [日瑋]. Originally from Daxing in Zhidai (present-day Beijing), although some sources say he was from Jiyuan County, He'nan Province, or from Chizhou (present-day Guichi County), Anhui Province. From an early age, he studied Xingyi and other arts from the art's founder, Ji Jike. However, according to the preface of the *Treatise on Xinyi Six Harmonies Boxing* by Dai Longbang, when Cao Jiwu was living in Qiupu (present-day Guichi County), Anhui Province, he studied Xinyi boxing with a student of Ji Jike's from the south surnamed Zheng.

After twelve years of arduous training, his art was refined and pure, and Cao was both skilled and courageous. In the governmental military tests he was "victorious with three firsts." According to both Zhou Jiannan's *Research on Xingyi Boxing* and the "Martial Worthies" section of the *Guichi County Gazetteer,* Cao Jiwu achieved first place in the Shuntian District examinations in the thirty-second year of the *kangxi* reign period (1693). The following *jiaxu* year, at the highest-level military examinations, he graduated first among all candidates; "the Emperor himself selected him as the top grade in the top class, and bestowed upon him the degree of *Jinshi.*"[19] Following this, Cao was made a third-degree imperial Bodyguard, and entered the Forbidden City.

In the thirty-sixth year [1697] he followed the Emperor to attack E'lu and, because of his diligent work, was repeatedly called before the court and honored with gifts of clothes, wine, and fruit. In the thirty-ninth year [1700] he was assigned as Adjunct of the Shanxi Province National Guard. Subsequently he received a special commission to become Vice-Commander of the Remote Pacification

Guard in Shaanxi Province, and was later promoted to Military Commissioner-in-Chief of Xing'an[20] Regional Command. At this time, there was great flooding on the Han River,[21] and [it is said that] Cao, while directing military troops in round-the-clock relief, suffered hypothermia and died at age thirty-six. Still another story has him retiring later in life and passing on his arts to many disciples in Chizhou and Luoyang.

Dai Longbang [戴龍邦] traveled from Shanxi to Chizhou, where Cao became his teacher. He studied with Cao for ten years, until his art was highly accomplished, and he later became the first generation of the Shanxi branch of Xingyi practitioners. Cao's other outstanding disciple, Ma Xueli [馬學禮], is considered the first generation of the He'nan branch Xingyi practitioners.[22]

Biography of Dai Longbang 戴龍邦
(1713–1802)

FOUNDER OF THE NORTHERN SCHOOL of Xinyi boxing. Pen-named Erlei [爾雷]. Originally from Qi County, Shanxi Province. From his youth he loved martial arts and studied the Chang-style boxing taught by his family. In the fourth year of the Qing *yongzheng* reign period (1726) when he was thirteen, Dai Longbang followed his father to Chizhou (present-day Guichi County), Anhui Province, to run a business. There he studied Xinyi Six Harmonies Boxing with Cao Jiwu, and after more than ten years of bitter training attained a deep understanding of its principles.

Dai traveled broadly in Shanxi, Anhui, and He'nan provinces, returning to Shanxi in the fifteenth year of the *qianlong* reign period (1750). While traveling through Luoyang in He'nan, he encountered and exchanged ideas with his school-brother Ma Xueli, which aided him greatly in further refining his art. With the help of Ma Xueli, Dai wrote the *Treatise on Xinyi Six Harmonies Boxing*. In practice, using the nature of the *Tuo* and *Tai*[23] as inspiration, he created the *Tuo* and *Tai* forms, adding these two animal forms to the existing ten forms of Xinyi boxing. Because he considered these to be secret skills, he taught them only to his son Wenliang [文亮] and to nephews Wenying [文英] and Wenxiong [文雄].[24]

49

Biography of Li Feiyu 李飛羽
(APPROX. 1809–1890)

MARTIAL ARTS PRACTITIONER; the founder of Hebei-style Xingyi boxing. Pen-named Laoneng [洛能]; also called Nengran [能然] or Laonong [老農]. Posthumously called Laoneng [老能]. Originally from Shen County, Hebei Province. From his youth he was fond of martial arts and first studied Hua-style Boxing.[25] According to "The Inscriptions of Che Yizhai's Tomb," Laoneng once traveled to Taigu in Shanxi Province on business, and it was there he heard that the Dai family of Xiaomu village, Qi County, was skilled in the art of Xinyi boxing. In order to study this art he subsequently moved to Qi County on the pretext of starting a farm and, after a series of unusually clever entreaties and by selecting various people to speak well of him and intercede on his behalf, he finally began studying Xinyi boxing as an official disciple of Dai Wenxiong (pen-named Erlü) in 1845. At this time Li was already thirty-seven years of age.

After ten years of hard practice and thorough research, he obtained the essential principles of Xinyi boxing. According to Sun Lutang's *True Tales of Boxing Intention,* Laoneng's skill "had reached the highest level." That year Li's sincere friend, an advanced military degree-holder of uncommon strength and skill in fighting arts, was residing in Qi County. One day the two were visiting when the degree-holder unexpectedly grabbed him from behind and tried to pick him up. Laoneng, however, had already jumped up and away from his grasp.

Around the time of the Qing *xianfeng* reign period (1856), Laoneng was asked to serve as house security for the local wealthy landowner Meng Boru, and it was after this that he began to take disciples. Locals including Che Yizhai (Yonghong) [車毅齋 (永宏)] and Song Shirong [宋世榮], as well as Liu Qilan [劉奇蘭], Guo Yunshen

[郭云深], and Liu Xiaolan [劉曉蘭], all of Hebei Province, were among those who studied his art. In order to spread Xinyi boxing, he combined his own teaching experience with his reorganization of the arts he had learned and thus created something new. From the hand-written version of Li's *Xingyi Boxing Manual,* we can see elements of theory and practice that were not present in the older *Treatise on Xinyi Six Harmonies Boxing* [by Dai Longbang] such as: when training splitting fist, he replaced the fist with a palm; in terms of internal skill, he initiated the idea of "three levels of *gongfu*"; and he proposed the idea of "practice to transform essence into *qi*, practice to transform *qi* into spirit, and practice to change spirit into nothingness." In addition, Li changed [the character] 'Xin' to 'Xing' and changed the art's name to Xingyi boxing.

During the process of teaching numerous students, Li gradually formed the idea that, while Xinyi boxing was its origin, Xingyi boxing was a complete and distinct system with its own skills and theory, and he made great contributions to this art. During his life, his students were numerous, and all were outstanding. Aside from those mentioned above, there were Li Jingzhai [李鏡齋], Liu Yuanheng [劉元亨], Zhang Shude [張树德], Bai Xiyuan [白西園], He Yongheng [贺永恒], Li Guangheng [李廣亨], Li Taihe [李太和], and Liu Zhihe [劉之和], among others. The students of his famous disciples spread throughout China and include Li Cunyi [李存義], Zhang Zhankui [張占魁], Wang Fuyuan [王福元], Wang Kuiyuan [王魁元], Xu Zhan'ao [許占鰲], and Qian Yantang [錢硯堂], among others.[26]

Biography of Guo Yunshen 郭云深
(1820–1901)

FAMED XINGYI MASTER. Also called Yusheng [峪生]. Originally from Shen County, Hebei Province. Although of short stature, Guo possessed a strong constitution and resolute will. As a youth he enthusiastically studied Shaolin boxing arts, but after practicing for several years had attained little. At the beginning of the Qing *tongzhi* reign period [1862], he met Li Feiyu, the founder of Hebei-style Xingyi, who explained to him that although the external forms of Xingyi were simple, its theory was profound. Subsequently Guo became Li's student and began studying Xingyi, first studying only *beng quan*, but later learning the complete art. [It is said that] when Li would travel by donkey to other places, Guo would follow behind him practicing *beng quan*. After twelve years of arduous study, Guo had not only fully grasped the principles of applying Xingyi and the mysteries of *ming jin, an jin,* and *hua jin,*[27] but also had attained the essence of broadsword, spear, straight-sword and staff, and excelled in using *beng quan*. During the third year of the *guangxu* reign period (1877) Guo began teaching at the Western Tombs, and then became martial arts instructor in the household of the Supervisor–in–Chief of the Six Mausolea, Tan Chongjie. Following this he served as instructor for the Qing Imperial House, teaching Zai Chun and Zai Lian, and later served as advisor to the Prefect of Zhengding Commandery, Qian Xicai, instructing his son Qian Yantang in boxing arts.

Yunshen esteemed chivalry and virtue towards people and detested evil. At the time, the bandit "Local Emperor" Dou Xianjun was harming people in the local villages. Guo killed him in their defense and then turned himself in to authorities. Knowing of Dou's wickedness, the magistrate only sentenced Guo to three years in jail on charges of manslaughter. Because both his feet and hands were shackled and his movement restricted, Guo could only practice "half-step *beng quan*" while jailed. As a result, his art became more supreme, and thus it was said that his "half-step *beng quan* strikes everywhere under heaven without match." After release from prison, Guo traveled widely throughout northeastern China and Hebei, Shandong, and He'nan provinces, all without encountering his equal [in boxing skill]. To test his ability, he would ask five strong young men to each press the points of wooden staffs against his abdomen which he would then rapidly expand, causing the five men to fly off and land on the ground more than a meter away. It was just as Sun Lutang wrote in his *True Tales of Boxing Intention*: "The principle behind all that Master [Guo] practiced was to make the abdomen completely full, and the mind completely empty. The form and appearance are heavy like Mt. Tai, but the body's movements are lively and nimble like a bird in flight."

Yunshen once traveled to the capital to compare his art with those of the famous Bagua practitioner Dong Haichuan and famous Taiji practitioner Yang Luchan. Without attempting to determine who was better or worse, they used their martial arts to establish friendship and became the sincerest of friends. Taking the best points and supplementing any shortcomings, they combined and integrated Taiji, Xingyi, and Bagua, and together made great contributions to the development of these arts.

Yunshen was educated in both martial arts and literature, and was also versed in military arts and poetry. He achieved much in his research into the principles and tenets of Xingyi, and in his later years retired to his hometown, where his experiences teaching were set forth in his *Explanation of the Xingyi Boxing Manual*. The students he instructed over the course of his life were quite numerous. Among the most famous are Li Kuiyuan, Qian Yantang, Wang Xiangyuan [王香元], Sun Lutang [孫禄堂], Xu Zhan'ao, and Wang Xiangzhai [王薌齋].[28]

Biography of Liu Qilan 劉奇蘭
(1819–1889)

FAMED XINGYI PRACTITIONER. Originally from Shen County, Hebei Province. From his youth he was fond of the fighting arts and was skilled in many empty-hand and armed arts. He was also very learned and was known as "The Distinguished Gentleman with Sagely Hands." Later he studied Xingyi with Li Feiyu. His attainments were quite profound, and he did not hold to the views of school and style, breaking the traditions of secretiveness and guardedness in teaching. He once raised troops for the gate guard in Shenzhou (present-day Shen County, Hebei Province), then later returned to his hometown.

Qilan was naturally broadminded, teaching his arts whole-heartedly, and his disciples were as numerous as clouds. Li Cunyi and Zhang Zhankui (among others) are examples of his lineage. Those continuing his art also included his son, Liu Dianchen [劉殿琛], as well as Liu Jintang [劉錦堂], Geng Chengxin [耿成信], Zhou Mingtai [周明泰], Tian Jingjie [田静傑], Liu Xiaolan,[29] Liu Fengchun [劉鳳春], and Liu Dekuan [劉德寬]. Dianchen later wrote *Plucking Out the Subtleties of Xingyi Boxing* to explain and spread his father's theory and art.

Liu Qilan and his school-brother Guo Yunshen made a special trip to the capital to call upon Dong Haichuan [董海川] at the residence of Prince Su and to exchange experiences with him. Because both [Guo and Dong] had expertise, they fought for three days without a victor emerging. This led from competition to a mutual admiration and an immediate friendship, and the encounter was spread as a popular story in the martial arts community at the time. After this it was said, "Xingyi and Bagua are united as one school." Thereafter people also acknowledged the proclamation of the "United Loyalty of the Seven Worthies" or "Sworn Alliance of the Nine Worthies" to "extinguish borders and not divide with limits." The "Seven Worthies" were Liu Qilan's famous disciples Li Cunyi, Zhang Zhankui, Geng Chengxin, Zhou Mingtai, and Liu Dekuan, and Dong Haichuan's famous disciples Cheng Tinghua [程廷華] and Yin Fu [尹福]. The "Nine Worthies," aside from the above-mentioned seven people, include Liu Qilan's famous disciples Tian Jingjie and Liu Fengchun.[30]

PORTRAIT OF LI CUNYI

Biography of Li Cunyi 李存義
(1847-1921)

MARTIAL ART PRACTITIONER. Originally named Cunyi [存毅], pen-named Sutang [肅堂]. Also pen-named Zhongyuan [忠元]. Originally from Shen County, Hebei Province. As a young man, his family was poor and he made his living in moving services. In his spare time, he practiced various arts and later traveled throughout Shandong, Hebei, and Shanxi searching for teachers. In midlife, he luckily happened upon Liu Qilan and began studying Xingyi boxing and Shaolin-style weapons. Afterward, he studied Xingyi with Guo Yunshen and Bagua with Dong Haichuan. He was also friends with Cheng Tinghua, and he excelled in his study of Bagua, reaching a deep understanding of the art, until Li Cunyi's name was known throughout the country.

In the twentieth year of the Qing *guangxu* reign (1894), he accepted a position as a martial arts instructor for the Qing army, later being promoted to Squad Leader under the Superior Security Group of the Zhejiang and Jiangxi Provinces Commander-in-Chief. Because he had little interest in being a career official, Li gave up his post and moved to Baoding, where he opened the Wantong Bodyguard Service, making his living in the bodyguard profession and teaching many students.

In the twenty-sixth year of the *guangxu* reign period, the Eight Allied Armies occupied Beijing. In order to resist this foreign insult, Cunyi led his students to join the Boxer Rebellion in the Tianjin area to fight against the invaders. He usually fought at the head of his troops carrying a single broadsword with which he bravely and fiercely killed many enemies. At the battle of Lao Long Kou in Tianjin, he inflicted heavy casualties on the enemy, and because of this his fame spread greatly and he was nicknamed "Single Saber Li" by his contemporaries. Later, Li gave up the bodyguard trade and concentrated on teaching. His famous students include Shang Yunxiang [尚雲祥], Sun Lutang,[31] Chu Guiting [諸桂亭], Ai Yongchun [艾永春], Huang Bonian [黃柏年], and the "Three Heroes of Dingxing"—Li Caiting [李彩亭],[32] [Li Yueting (李躍亭), and Li Wenting (李文亭)].

In the third year of the Qing *xuantong* reign period (1911), in order to inspire the spirit of the masses and to resist the influence of the principles of Japanese *Bushido*, Li established (with the help of Ye Yunbiao [葉雲表], Ma Fengtu [馬鳳圖], Li Ruidong [李瑞東], and Zhang Zhankui) the Chinese Martial Artists Assembly. Ye Yunbiao acted as President, and Li acted as Vice-President and Chief Instructor. Among others, they invited the famous teachers Li Shuwen [李書文], Huo Diange [霍殿閣], and Hao Enguang [郝恩光] to be instructors. This Assembly had a considerable influence at the time, and a sub-branch was even established in Japan. Li accepted the invitation of the Generals Wang Zhixiang and Ma Zizhen to serve as Martial Arts Instructor for the Army Corps, and in September 1918, he and Zhang Zhankui led more than ten of his students, including Li Jianqiu [李劍秋] and Han Muxia [韓慕俠], to attend the World Martial Arts Competition in Beijing, where Li Cunyi defeated the arrogant Russian strongman Kangtaier. Later he assumed a position at the Shanghai Jingwu Academy, and also taught at Shanghai Nanyang Public College (the former name of present-day Shanghai Jiaotong University). Following Huo Yuanjia, Li taught Xingyi boxing in Shanghai, and Hebei-style Xingyi boxing flourished in southern China. Li's writings include *A Fighting Arts Instruction Manual, A Compendium of True Xingy,* and *The Essentials of Northern and Southern Fighting Arts.*[33]

Biography of Sun Fuquan 孫福全
(1860–1933)

MARTIAL ARTS PRACTITIONER. Founder of Sun-Wu-style Taiji,[34] but also skilled in Xingyi and Bagua. Pen-named Lutang [禄堂]; late in life he took the style-name Hanzhai [涵斋]. Originally from Wan County (present-day Wangdu County), Hebei Province. As a youth he was naturally intelligent and his disposition gentle. He first studied martial arts under Li Kuiyuan, and after several years of focusing primarily on Xingyi boxing had learned all that Li could teach. He continued his studies by obtaining the essence of Xingyi from his Grand-teacher Guo Yunshen, often accompanying Guo in his travels to other provinces, and thus greatly increasing his knowledge and experience. He also received instruction from such elder-generation practitioners as Che Yizhai, Song Shirong, Liu Qilan, and Bai Xiyuan, and thus his Xingyi skill became completely accomplished. Later he traveled to the capital and studied the essentials of Bagua from Cheng Tinghua, fully grasping its mysteries. Because his martial skill was deep, he enjoyed the praise of all the capital's [martial arts] masters.

Lutang's appearance was very thin, and his frame small, but his movements were lively and nimble, and so he was called "living monkey Sun Lutang." Later Sun met the famous Taiji practitioner Hao Weizhen [郝維禎], through whose instruction he acquired the subtleties of Wu-style Taiji. In Sun's later years, when his skill had become refined—able to create sublime transformations and adapt his movements to the situation without fixed rules and thus synthesize with thorough comprehension—he combined the essential points of Xingyi, Bagua, and Taiji to create Sun-style Taiji. Lutang read the *Book of Changes* and the *Elixir Classic* and used these to explain boxing theory, establishing the system of thought in martial studies that "boxing must be united with the Dao," as well as the principles of "the three fists" uniting as one, and "the pre- and post-heaven Bagua uniting." The unique characteristics [of Sun-style Taiji] include "advancing and retreating follow one another, one must have a root when stepping and pull back when retreating"; "movements should be relaxed, open and lively, and one's agility natural"; "in practice one must clearly differentiate solid and empty in the two feet, continuously without cease like floating clouds or running water"; and "when changing directions, one should always use both 'opening' and 'closing' to meet." Thus this art was also called "Opening and Closing Lively-Step Taiji Boxing." The Xingyi that Sun taught also contained some of the essence of both Bagua and Taiji.

Between 1915 and 1925, Sun secluded himself away to research and concentrate on writing, altogether producing five specialized works: *The Study of Form-Intention Boxing; The Study of Eight Diagrams Palm; The Study of Supreme Ultimate Boxing; The Study of Eight-Diagrams Broadsword;* and *True Tales of Boxing Intention.* His writings were rich, and started the flow of martial arts-specialized writing. Lutang's martial virtue was lofty and his martial skill unsurpassed. Although he was not once defeated during his lifetime of comparing skills with others, he was never conceited and always emphasized that "the purpose of cultivating martial arts is to develop one's disposition."

At the end of the Qing Dynasty, at the request of Xu Shichang,[35] Sun became an Internal Investigator in Fengtian, where he later was promoted to District Magistrate. In 1918, he served as Vice-Commandant in the Presidential Office, then subsequently was made a Commissioner, and later accepted a post as a Major in the army. In 1928, he accepted an appointment as Wudang-Arts Bureau Chief at the Central Martial Arts Academy, and later served simultaneously as the Vice Director and Head of Instructional Affairs for the Jiangsu Province National Arts Academy. Late in life he returned to his hometown, and passed away without sickness. His students are numerous and among the most famous are his disciples Sun Jianyun [孫劍雲], Sun Cunzhou [孫存周], Qi Gongbo [齊公博], Sun Zhenchuan [孫振川], Sun Zhendai [孫振岱], and Hu Fengshan [胡風山].[36]

PORTRAIT OF SUN FUQUAN

PORTRAIT OF SHANG YUNXIANG

Biography of Shang Yunxiang 尚雲祥
(1864–1937)

AMED XINGYI PRACTITIONER. Pen-named Jiting [霽庭] or, in some sources, Jiting [集亭]. Originally from Leling County, Shandong Province. As a youth, he traveled with his father to do business in Beijing, where he developed an interest in martial arts. He first studied Gongli boxing[37] from Ma Dayi. Once, when testing his skills, he was defeated by the Xingyi boxing practitioner Li Zhihe [李志和][38] and realized that Xingyi boxing was an exceptional art. Thereupon he became a disciple of Li Cunyi and practiced Xingyi boxing diligently.

After his art was skillful, he took a position as inspector with the military body of the five cities, and later served as head of house security for the Qing Court Eunuch and Area Military Commander-in-Chief Li. Because his Xingyi skills were outstanding, Shang aroused the interest of Guo Yunshen, from whom he received secret teachings, and his skills became even more refined, especially his foot-skill, which earned him the nickname "Iron-leg Buddha." He also learned the essence of Guo Yunshen's *beng quan* and became skilled in this as well. After studying with Guo Yunshen, Shang was also nicknamed [as was Guo himself] by many as "the one whose half-step *beng quan* strikes everywhere under Heaven." Shang once used the *Tai* form to defeat Miyun County's "Spirit Sand Palm" Feng Luozheng. Shang used "Split grab connect wrap capture" to defeat a spear-stab towards his throat by big-spear practitioner Ma Xiu from Shunyi County, also known as the "Iron Arhat" of He'nan Province. He soundly defeated and assisted authorities in the capture of the great thief of Tongzhou, "Big Boss Eighth Kang" Kang Tianxin, a skilled fighter versed in lightness skill who had harmed many in the area. After this, Shang Yunxiang's fame spread throughout China. His disciples include Jin Yunting, Zhao Keli [趙克禮], Sun Mengzhi [孫夢之], Xu Yuzhi [許羽之], and Li Wenbin [李文彬].[39]

Endnotes

¹ 宮保, the position of tutor to the heir-apparent under the Qing Dynasty. Also sometimes used as an honorary government title with no real authority or responsibility.

² The posthumous title of the Song Dynasty general Yue Fei.

³ 五行拳, literally, Five Element Boxing.

⁴ 元氣, original or congenital *qi*.

⁵ *Mengzi*, Book 2, part I, chapter 2, section 9. As Charles Muller writes: "The Chinese ideograph ch'i originally means 'air,' especially breath. Through Mencius' usage, and the usage of later Taoists, martial artists, and the Neo-Confucian school, its meaning becomes quite enhanced. Here ch'i, as breath, is understood as the vital connection between body and mind. It is the life-force which animates the body to greater or lesser degrees, depending upon its cultivation toward the vigor and vitality of the individual. In the terms with which Mencius describes it, ch'i can be compared to the *prana* of some Indian yogic systems, which can be cultivated through breath control and various other yogic practices. "One of the most relevant points that Mencius makes in regard to the cultivation of ch'i is that this cultivation is dependent, more than anything else, on the uninterrupted practice of Righteousness."

Muller's translation of sections 9-16 is as follows:

> Ch'ou asked, "Will you please tell me about your 'mental stability' in relation to Kao Tzu's 'mental stability'?"
>
> Mencius replied, "Kao Tzu says that what cannot be attained through words should not be sought for in the mind, and that what cannot be attained in the mind should not be sought for through the *ch'i*. This latter proposition is correct, but the first one is not. The *will* is the director of the *ch'i*, and the *ch'i* is something that permeates the body. So the will is primary and the *ch'i* is secondary. Therefore, it is said: 'Hold on to your will; do not scatter your *ch'i*.'"
>
> Ch'ou said, "You just said that the will is primary; and the *ch'i* is secondary. Now you say, 'hold on to your will; don't scatter your *ch'i*.' Why do you say this?"
>
> Mencius said, "The will influences the *ch'i* and the *ch'i*

influences the will. For instance, jumping and running, though most directly concerned with the *ch'i*, also have an effect on the mind."

"May I ask in what it is that you are superior?"

"I understand language, and I am good at nourishing my vast *ch'i*."

"What do you mean by 'vast *ch'i*'?"

"That is difficult to explain. *Ch'i* can be developed to great levels of quantity and stability by correctly nourishing it and not damaging it, to the extent that it fills the space between Heaven and Earth. In developing *ch'i*, if you are connected with Righteousness and the Tao, you will never be in want of it. It is something that is produced by accumulating Righteousness, and is not something that you can grab from superficial attempts at Righteousness. If you act without mental composure, you will become *ch'i*-starved.

"Therefore I would say that Kao Tzu has not yet understood Righteousness, since he regards it as something external. You must be willing to work at it, understanding that you cannot have precise control over it. You can't forget about it, but you can't force it to grow, either.

"You don't want to be like the man from Sung. There was a man from Sung who was worried about the slow growth of his crops and so he went and yanked on them to accelerate their growth. Empty-headed, he returned home and announced to his people: 'I am so tired today. I have been out stretching the crops.' His son ran out to look, but the crops had already withered. Those in the world who don't 'help their crops by pulling' are few indeed. There are also those who regard all effort as wasteful and don't even weed their crops. But those who think they can hurry their growth along by forcing it are not only not helping their *ch'i*, but actually harming it!"

[6] *Mengzi,* Book 2, part I, chapter 2, section 11.

[7] As noted in the Digital Dictionary of Buddhism, http://www.acmuller.net/ddb/index.html, the *Mahāprajñāpāramitā-sūtra* 般若波羅蜜多經, or a general term for the sutras that teach the perfection of wisdom, i.e., emptiness 空. Most likely referring to the 'Heart of Wisdom Sutra,' a widely known and commonly chanted Buddhist text whose core tenet is that "emptiness is form and form is emptiness."

[8] The clear and turbid fluids. For a detailed discussion, see Maciocia, Giovanni. *The Foundations of Chinese Medicine.* London: Churchill Livingstone, 1989, p. 35.

9 The eye of the fist.

10 人, a description of the position of the feet. Usually seen in Xingyi texts as *ba-shape feet,* 八字形.

11 A slightly forward-weighted twisted horse stance.

12 十字步, also called 剪步. A step through with a following step.

13 Although the same phrase as described in Note 11 above, here it denotes the movement of the legs as they come together.

14 During the Song, one *jin* was equal to 633 grams—thus, a 418-pound bow.

15 During the Song, one *dan* was equal to 75.96 kilograms—thus, a 1337-pound crossbow.

16 A military formation with two wings of skilled cavalry facing in at the sides of the main infantry, looking like the heads of two canes.

17 *Zhongguo Wushu Baike Quanshu,* edited by Shan Zhang (Beijing: Zhongguo Baike Quanshu Chubanshe, 1998), pp. 531–532.

18 *Zhongguo Wushu Baike Quanshu,* p. 538.

19 "Advanced Gentleman," the highest rank under the old examination system.

20 A city in northeast Jiangxi Province.

21 A tributary of the Yangtze River in Shanxi Province.

22 *Zhongguo Wushu Baike Quanshu,* p. 541.

23 鼉, water-lizard, and 鴼 the *Tai* bird, sometimes translated as phoenix.

24 *Zhongguo Wushu Baike Quanshu,* pp. 542–543.

25 花拳

26 *Zhongguo Wushu Baike Quanshu,* pp. 544–545.

27 明劲，暗劲，化劲 The three principles of internal power.

28 *Zhongguo Wushu Baike Quanshu,* p. 547.

29 A probable error. Liu Xiaolan was Liu Qilan's school brother, not student, and no sources list a student by that name.

30 *Zhongguo Wushu Baike Quanshu,* pp. 546–547.

31 Though Sun Lutang studied widely with many prominent martial artists, most biographies do not list Li Cunyi as one of his teachers.

32 Most sources list Li Haiting [李海亭].

33 *Zhongguo Wushu Baike Quanshu,* p. 548.

34 孙武太极拳

35 A prominent Qing-Dynasty official and, later, political reformer under the Republican Government.

36 *Zhongguo Wushu Baike Quanshu,* p. 550. 37 功力拳

38 Li Zhihe's name does not appear on any of the common lineage charts, though he is presumably a student of Li Cunyi.

39 *Zhongguo Wushu Baike Quanshu,* p. 50.

Bibliography

Digital Dictionary of Buddhism. Chief Editor, Charles Muller. Retrieved 4/22/2003 from the DDB website: http://www.acmuller.net/ddb/index.html>.

Hucker, Charles O. *A Dictionary of Official Titles in Imperial China*. Stanford, CA: Stanford University Press, 1985.

Jiang Jinshi [江金石]. *Xingyi Quan Rumen* [形意拳入門]. Tainan, Taiwan: Xinhong Chubanshe [信宏出版社], 1999.

Liang Shou-Yu and Jwing-Ming Yang. *Xingyiquan: Theory, Applications, Fighting Tactics and Spirit*. Boston: YMAA Publication Center, 2002.

Maciocia, Giovanni. *The Foundations of Chinese Medicine*. London: Churchill Livingstone, 1989.

McNeil, James W. *Hsing-I*. Burbank, CA: Unique Publications.

Miller, Dan, and Tim Cartmell. *Xing Yi Nei Gong: Xing Yi Health Maintenance and Internal Strength Development*. Pacific Grove, CA: High View Publications, 1994.

Muller, Charles. *Mencius (Selections)*. June 2000. Retrieved 4/22/2003 from the Resources for East Asian Language and Thought website: http://www.human.toyogakuen-u.ac.jp/~acmuller/contao/mencius.htm.

Pa Kua Chang Journal, 1994, Vol. 4, #3.

Sun Lutang. *Xing Yi Quan Xue: The Study of Form-Mind Boxing*. Translated by Albert Liu, edited by Dan Miller. Pacific Grove, CA: High View Publications, 1993.

Xue, Dian [薛顛]. *Xingyi Quanshu Jiang Yi* [形意拳術講義]. Taibei, Taiwan: Yiwen Chubanshe [逸文出版社], 2000.

Zhongguo Wushu Baike Quanshu [中國武術百科全書]. Edited by Shan Zhang [張山]. Beijing: Zhongguo Baike Quanshu Chubanshe [中國百科全書出版社], 1998.

About the Translator

JOHN GROSCHWITZ began his martial arts training in 1995 with the study of Northern Shaolin. He began training in Xingyi Quan in 1996 and is currently an Assistant Instructor in Xingyi with the North American Tang Shou Tao Association. In addition to continuing study in the above arts, he has also studied Lanshou Quan, Gao-style Bagua Zhang, Water Boxing, Yang-style Taiji Quan, and various systems of Qi Gong, in the U.S. and Mainland China.

John has studied Chinese language and literature for more than ten years and has worked as a translator, interpreter, and lecturer. After graduating from the University of California, Berkeley, in 1996 with a B.A. in Chinese, he translated freelance and interpreted for various organizations, including the San Francisco Art Institute, U.C. Berkeley, and Tibet House New York. In 2001, he received an M.A. from Stanford University in East Asian Studies with an emphasis in Chinese Literature.